I Can Write Instructions

Anita Ganeri

Chicago, Illinois

www.capstonepub.com
Visit our website to find out more information about Heinemann-Raintree books.

To order:
☎ Phone 800-747-4992
💻 Visit www.capstonepub.com
to browse our catalog and order online.

© 2013 Heinemann Library
an imprint of Capstone Global Library, LLC
Chicago, Illinois

All rights reserved. No part of this publication may be reproduced or transmitted in any form or by any means, electronic or mechanical, including photocopying, recording, taping, or any information storage and retrieval system, without permission in writing from the publisher.

Edited by Daniel Nunn, Rebecca Rissman, and Sian Smith
Designed by Victoria Allen
Picture research by Elizabeth Alexander
Original illustrations © Capstone Global Library Ltd 2013
Illustrated by Victoria Allen and Darren Lingard
Production by Victoria Fitzgerald

Originated by Capstone Global Library Ltd
Printed and bound in China by Leo Paper Products Ltd

Hardback ISBN: 978 1 4329 6934 9
Paperback ISBN: 978 1 4329 6941 7

16 15 14 13 12
10 9 8 7 6 5 4 3 2 1

Library of Congress Cataloging-in-Publication Data
Cataloging-in-Publication data is available at the Library of Congress.

Acknowledgments
We would like to thank the following for permission to reproduce photographs and artworks: Alamy p. 7 (© Nick Gregory); iStockphoto pp. 12 (© Scott Griessel), 14 (© ac_bnphotos); Shutterstock pp. 4 (© AISPIX), 5 (© Milos Luzanin), 8 (© Gelpi), 9 (© Golden Pixels LLC), 10 (© Noam Armonn), 13 (© OtnaYdur), 15 (© DVARG), 19 (© spaxiax), 20 (© BW Folsom), 21 (© Madlen), 21 (© Nataliia Natykach), 22 (© Terrie L. Zeller), 23 (© wacpan), 23 (© Nayuco), 24 (© Fotokostic), 25 (© Oleksii Sagitov), 26 (© Somjade Boonyarat), 27 (© Igor Dutina); Superstock p. 6 (© Onoky).

Every effort has been made to contact copyright holders of material reproduced in this book. Any omissions will be rectified in subsequent printings if notice is given to the publisher.

Disclaimer
All the Internet addresses (URLs) given in this book were valid at the time of going to press. However, due to the dynamic nature of the Internet, some addresses may have changed, or sites may have changed or ceased to exist since publication. While the author and publisher regret any inconvenience this may cause readers, no responsibility for any such changes can be accepted by either the author or the publisher.

Contents

What Is Writing? 4
What Are Instructions? .6
Different Instructions 8
Good Instructions 10
Writing Style 12
Making Lists 14
Adding Pictures 16
In the Right Order 18
Making a Sandwich 20
Making a Birthday Card 22
Playing Soccer 24
Growing a Sunflower .26
Top Tips for Writing Instructions 28
Glossary *30*
Find Out More *31*
Index *32*

Some words are shown in bold, **like this**. You can find out what they mean in the glossary on page 30.

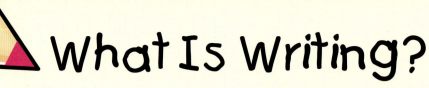

What Is Writing?

When you put words on paper or on a computer screen, you are writing. Learning to write clearly is important so that your readers can understand what you mean.

What do you like writing about?

These instructions tell you how to wash a piece of clothing.

There are many different types of writing. This book is about instructions. Instructions are a type of **nonfiction**. This means that they are about facts.

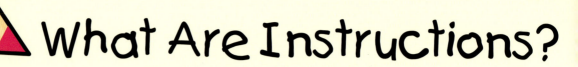

What Are Instructions?

Instructions are **step-by-step** guides that explain how to do or make something. This might be something such as baking a cake or playing a game.

You follow instructions when you are cooking.

Some instructions can be difficult to follow.

Instructions need to be clear and simple, so that the reader can follow them. Before you start writing, think about what needs to be done, and in what order.

Different Instructions

There are lots of different types of instructions. If you want to learn how to play a musical instrument, you need to follow some instructions.

You need instructions to learn how to play the guitar.

Instructions help you learn to take care of a pet.

You might also be given instructions about how to stay safe, find your way, or make models. A veterinarian might give you instructions for caring for a new pet.

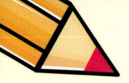

Good Instructions

When you are writing instructions, think about the title. It should tell the reader what he or she is going to make or do. Instructions should be short and snappy.

How to brush your teeth

This title tells the reader the aim of the instructions.

Think about what you need to say in your instructions. Make sure that they are in the right order. Use short, clear **sentences** so that your reader does not get confused.

Here are some things to include when you are writing instructions.

Things to include

- title
- list of **equipment** needed
- list of steps
- **diagram**

Writing Style

Use bossy **verbs** to write your instructions. These give orders and tell readers what to do. They make your instructions easier to understand.

Bossy verbs
jump
cut
stir
draw
fold

Here are some bossy verbs. Can you think of any more?

Write the steps in the correct order. You can use words called **time clauses** to help you. Look at the list of time clauses below.

Can you think of any more time clauses?

first

next

then

after

finally

Making Lists

Write down the **equipment**, tools, or **ingredients** that the reader needs. Write this as a list. You can use **bullet points** to make the list clear for your reader.

Making gelatin

You will need:

- gelatin powder or cubes
- boiling water
- a jug
- a bowl
- a wooden spoon

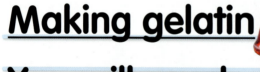

Make sure that you have not forgotten anything.

Make a list of the steps that the reader needs to follow. Make sure that they are in the right order. You can use numbers to make the order clear.

Remember to add any safety warnings to your instructions—for example, "Ask an adult to help boil the water."

1. Put the gelatin powder or cubes in the bowl
2. Pour the water in and stir.

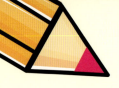

Adding Pictures

You can add pictures or **diagrams** to make your instructions clearer. It is useful to number these so that they match the list of steps.

> Here you can see some of the steps in making a robot.

Making a model robot

1. Stick a small box on top of a large box. This is the robot's head.

2. Stick on cardboard tubes for its arms and legs.

If you are telling the reader how to make something, show a picture of the finished item. Add labels to explain what the different parts are.

Draw lines from the labels to the correct parts of your diagram.

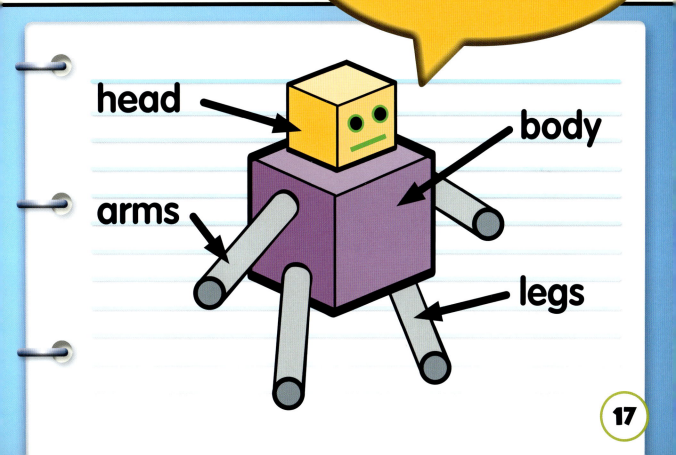

In the Right Order

Read the instructions below. They tell you how to wash your hands, but they are mixed up in the wrong order.

These instructions make no sense.

Put soap on your hands.

Dry your hands on the towel.

Rinse the soap off.

Turn on the faucet.

Rub your hands together.

Turn off the faucet.

Wet your hands.

Can you sort the instructions out and put them in the right order? You can number them to make the order clear.

Add numbers to the instructions.

1. Turn on the faucet.
2. Wet your hands.
3. Put soap on your hands.
4. Rub your hands together.
5. Rinse the soap off.
6. Turn off the faucet.
7. Dry your hands on the towel.

Making a Sandwich

Try writing some instructions for making a jelly sandwich. Start with the title and a list of things that the reader will need.

Use **bullet points** for your list.

Make a sandwich

You will need:
- **bread**
- **butter**
- **jelly**
- **knife**
- **plate**

Write down your **step-by-step** instructions. Make sure that they are in the right order. Here is the first one to start you off.

Can you write the rest of the steps?

1. **Put two slices of bread on the plate.**
2. **???**
3. **???**

Making a Birthday Card

Making a birthday card is fun. Can you write some instructions for making a card? Keep them simple and easy to follow.

Find out if your instructions work by asking someone to try them out.

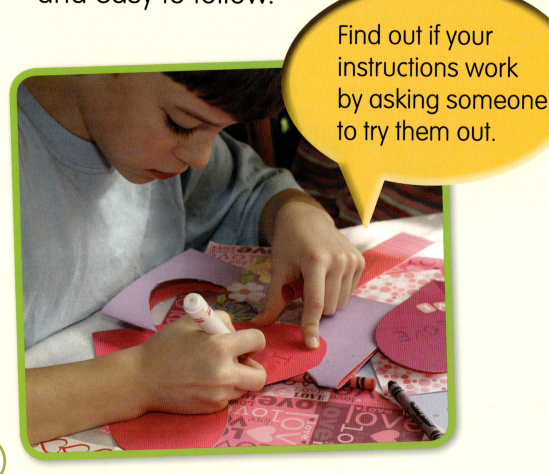

It can help if you make your own card first. Then you can write down the steps you used to make it. Here are some "bossy" words to help you.

Can you use these words in your instructions?

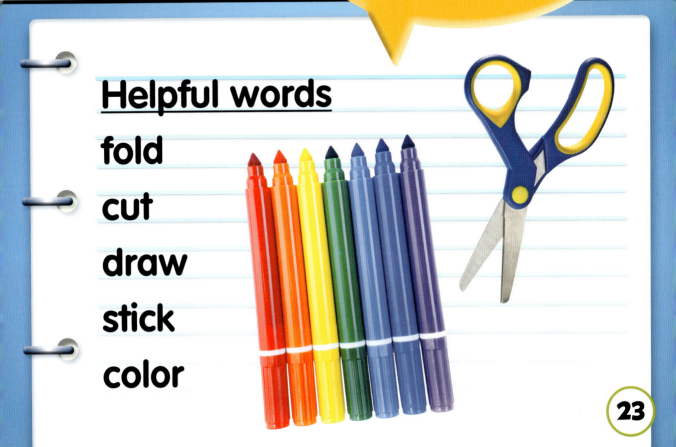

Helpful words
fold
cut
draw
stick
color

Playing Soccer

Imagine that you are writing to your **pen pal**. He or she has never played soccer before. Write some instructions to explain how you play soccer.

How do you tell someone how to play soccer?

Think of all the things that you need to explain. For example, you need to say how many players there are on a team, how long to play, and how to win a game.

Here are some words to help you.

Helpful words
team
ball
field
goal
kick

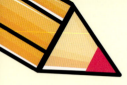
Growing a Sunflower

On these two pages, you can read some instructions for growing a sunflower. Look at the "You will need" list. Is anything missing from it?

Grow a sunflower

You will need:

- **a pot**
- **soil**
- **water**

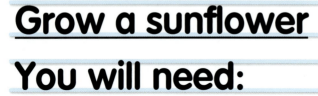

The answer is: a sunflower seed!

Look at the steps below. They are mixed up. Can you put them in the right order? Can you think of any more steps?

You could add a final step: Water your seed every day.

Push the seed into the soil.

Fill the pot with soil almost to the top.

Water the soil.

Cover the seed with soil.

Top Tips for Writing Instructions

1. Always read your instructions through to make sure that they are in the right order and make sense.

2. Imagine that you are explaining things to an alien from another planet who has never done them before.

3. Look at other instructions, such as those on packages or cans of food, in recipe books, on computer games, and so on. It will help you in your writing.

4. Keep your **sentences** short so that they are easy to understand. If you use difficult words, make sure that you explain them.

5. Add any safety tips to your instructions. For example, if you are telling someone how to make a sandwich, he or she needs to be careful when using a knife.

6. Look at a board game or jigsaw puzzle. What do you think of the instructions? Are they simple and clear? Can you follow them easily?

7. Make your writing style friendlier by saying "You…," or more **formal** by just using bossy words to give orders.

8. Keep practicing! Writing is like learning to ride your bike or roller skating. You need to keep practicing.

Glossary

bullet point small dot that is used instead of a number in a list

diagram picture showing how something works

equipment things you might need to make something—for example scissors, glue, and cardboard to make a model

formal language that is correct and follows the rules

ingredients list of the different foods you need to make something, such as a cake

nonfiction writing that is about real people or things

pen pal friend you write to, even though you may never have met him or her

sentence group of words that makes sense on its own

step-by-step explaining something in order, one step after the other

time clause word or words that say when something happened

verb doing, or action, word

Find Out More

Books

Benke, Karen. *Rip the Page! Adventures in Creative Writing*. Boston: Trumpeter, 2010.

Ganeri, Anita. *Getting to Grips with Grammar* series. Chicago: Heinemann Library, 2012.

Internet Sites

Facthound offers a safe, fun way to find Internet sites related to this book. All of the sites on Facthound have been researched by our staff.

Here's all you do:

Visit www.facthound.com

Type in this code: 9781432969349

Index

board games 29
bossy words 12, 23, 29
bullet points 14, 20

caring for a pet 9
cooking 6, 14–15

diagrams 11, 16–17

equipment 11, 14

formal writing style 29
friendly writing style 29

growing a sunflower 26–27

ingredients 14

jigsaw puzzles 29

labels 17
lists 11, 14–15

making a birthday card 22–23
making a sandwich 20–21, 29

nonfiction 5
numbers 15, 19

pen pals 24
pictures 16–17
playing music 8
playing soccer 24–25
practicing 29

right order 11, 13, 15, 18–19, 27, 28

safety warnings 15, 29
sentences 11, 28
step-by-step guides 6, 21

time clauses 13
titles 10
top tips 28
trying out instructions 22

verbs 12

writing (what it is) 4
writing style 12–13, 29